Prisoner of the Br

Bryce Walton

Alpha Editions

This edition published in 2024

ISBN 9789362517395

Design and Setting By
Alpha Editions
www.alphaedis.com
Email - info@alphaedis.com

Prisoner of the Brain-mistress

There are all kinds of men labeled with all sorts and degrees of psycho tags. For what it's worth, I have always been primarily motivated by an insatiable urge for action.

I have always awakened with faculties sharp and eyes clear, ready for any emergency of which there are plenty in these chaotic years of social adjustment from the Twentieth to the Twenty-fifth Century. This awakening I knew would exceed in magnitude any I had known. I knew I was in a place to which the little alien man had brought me.

I was stretched out on a smooth cold table of metal. I was also aware of a contraption of unknown purpose clamped about my skull, and my entire store of bodily faculties seemed vitally prepared for any eventuality, as though steeling itself for a subconsciously preconceived super-human effort.

I still hesitated about opening my eyes. It wasn't from physical fear which I have learned to convert into mental and physical energy. There was a fear of that alienness. Alien was the word for the little man with the bulbous head and crinkled little face of a premature child.

I knew that his outer dress and hairless, swollen and blue-veined skull, and the invisible electronic force that had brought us here, were all of some other time, world, dimension, or something of all three.

It wasn't exceptional on my part to be thinking of such fantastic possibilities in such a calm and detached a manner. Nothing seems fantastic anymore to a Twenty-fifth Centurian. Nothing. What we have not actually seen practiced through the marvels of chemistry and electronics, we have been trained to believe possible. We have two great goals facing us around the corner of probability—an Elixir of Life from some bio-chemical laboratory, and a ship constructed for an ultimate landing on a distant star.

But first, we must readjust the various political factions which prevent integration of human potential.

The last effort is the gigantic one. All other sciences have advanced beyond the science of society which is still infantile, but learning to walk more or less alone. The goal of global social integration is in sight, but the battle will still be long and difficult. This all leads to the body of this story—to the World-City of Mohln, to which the Scientist, Draken, brought me for the fulfillment of a grandiose and necessary, but horribly destructive destiny.

When the Fascisti wormed their way underground after their crushing defeat by the forces of World Democracy, after the close of that episode of evolutionary birth pangs called World War II, they created a small, evil and powerful recalcitrant force of reaction, seeking to regain minority control over the Earth Mass. Their threat is their secrecy. They never work openly; they are too small in number; but their acts of sabotage and political intrigue is disheartening at times, and a constant threat to our Administrative balance.

As elected Commander of the International Secret Police, my sole duty is to combat the specially trained cult of sabateurs of our democratic World-State, the Black Spartans.

Somehow that night—I've never been able to find the leak—two of them gained the top of my apartment building and were hiding on the roof landing as I stepped out to enter my jet-car.

There was no warning, no challenge. Their aim was simply to burn me out. Some well-trained intuitive sense threw me in a long dive forward and sidewise as the shaft of deadly heat crackled past and smoked beside my outstretched hand.

My E-special blaster was out and ready even as I hit the fine plastic mesh of the roof. I twisted over and burned a swath in their direction. I came up to one knee, keeping their area lanced with rays, then to my feet, going to one side and trying to distinguish their black plastic suits from the shadows.

A form stumbled out of the thick dark. It was half bent forward, grasping its middle. I smelled scorched flesh and knew he must be mortally injured, but I couldn't afford to underestimate the fanatical power of a Spartan.

He was still coming at me, so I burned him again, watched him crumble and sag. That was an error. The other Spartan, who was still somewhere back in the shadows of the collonade, blasted my arm, burning it half through. I watched my fingers curl and my E-special fall out and away slowly as in a dream.

There wasn't pain, physical pain. There was sheer mental anguish as I visualized myself closing my career of duty for the World-State, a failure. I knew what they wanted with my corpse. Dead, my cerebrum would be removed, activated, and its mental storage released through electronic recorders the Spartan scientists had developed. They preferred a brain taken from death as there was no slightest difficulty from conscious or even subconscious resistance.

But the Spartan couldn't burn me without a parting voice. His egomania demanded that I see and hear the power that had defeated me. He came out of the shadows, a black muscled melodramatic outline.

"Goodby," he slurred in a thick accent. "For a reputed great man, you employ pathetic guards. Your force is growing weak and negligent, Allinger. Soon our long wait and our long fight will reach its victorious end, even as you reach your shameful end now."

The Spartan tensed his blaster and I leaped straight into it, desperately, because I had nothing to lose.

I never got to him, and his blaster never got to me. I hit something painfully and bounced off. My arm was a lump of burning agony as I thudded to the roof, stunned by an impact with an invisible barrier.

The Spartan was discharging his blaster at me, but the power rebounding flung him to his knees. The blaster was knocked over the side of the roof-landing, and the Spartan staggered to his feet again, and weaved back.

Then, abruptly, his eyes bulged with awe that changed to terror. He backed away, staring, not at me, but at something beside me. Then the Spartan disappeared suddenly. I heard a faint *whirring* that rose up and faded rapidly. For an instant I followed the sound of the jet-car as it receded toward the red moon outlining the archaic structure of the Golden Gate Bridge, then I turned to see what had saved my life. It had been prolonged at least.

I hadn't been at all surprised to see the little man appear on the private jet-car landing of my San Francisco apartment. There had been no sound, only coruscating shifting hues of light that materialized him, not like the magic of old, but with all the magnificent and unlimited magic of science.

He stood there juggling the huge silver globe like a bubble toy, but one that certainly could never burst. His long, delicate arms and legs and torso couldn't have lifted twenty pounds without straining. The silver sphere must be elevated by unknown forces of its own.

The little man's body, only a bit more than bone tightly stretched over with transparent, form fitting material, swayed toward me. The pinched up, chalk face in the midst of that bulging head studied me with enigmatic lack of expression that was extremely disconcerting. I could read plenty of purpose behind the blankness. So much elaborate ritual demanded proportionate purpose.

The ancient bulky structure of the Bridge twinkled its lights against the night sky behind the little man. Or was it the twitching of my eyes? I was preparing for a run over to the Federal Building for a meeting of the Pacific

Defense Zone of the International Peace Maintenance Fleet, but, important as that meeting was to be, I had forgotten it completely.

His voice was nasal, squeaky, and somehow contemptuous. It was halting, too, difficult to follow. I doubted if he had ever employed the International symbols before. In fact, I intuitively knew that he was either not of my time at all, or not of my world.

"I have studied the psychology of all potential men for the task that is to follow. I have chosen you, Ivan Allinger."

"Should I be flattered?"

I studied him, but could reach no conclusion.

The face puckered more. "Flattered?" The meaning of the word seemed to escape him for a moment. "Perhaps. It is a great task. I have not chosen you because of your physical attributes alone, although they seem exceptional enough. Your ideological background will synchronize perfectly with the job that you must do in Mohln."

"Mohln?"

"It is another world. A future and far distant one."

"You are from some future time? Really?"

"Yes. Mohln is another planet of this system, to which your descendants will migrate in a length of time you would label one million years. Our greatest scientist, the atavistic female, Jokan, demanded that I go back into the past of the race and seek out an object for her laboratory experiments."

I accepted him as he presented himself, which is always advisable under such circumstances. "I'm afraid that doesn't sound inviting at all," I explained. "A guinea pig of some sort for future scientific probing. Sorry." I started away, though I knew he could stop me when he pleased. It was a test. But he stopped me with a word.

"Wait, Ivan."

I turned. "Yes?"

"My reasons for choosing you are different from Jokan's reasons. Let me explain." He tottered toward me weakly on his spindly legs. I towered over him as he squinted up into my face.

"There are many reasons why I cannot allow your refusal," he said. "One great reason that ties you with destiny."

I tried to escape then, feeling that he was right. I knew that a series of unimaginable events were twisting me into cosmic circumstances. Circumstances too gigantic to even excite amazement or disbelief, only stunned passivity. I wasn't able to execute an about face or the lifting of one leg that might possibly have sent me beyond the range of the little man's potentiality.

I had forgotten the silver sphere which bobbed beside him as a monstrous toy might. It began to glow and expand into a great bulb of incandescence, and it caught me immediately and paralyzed me, and sucked me into realms of cosmology beyond the wildest imaginings of all the Einsteins. I actually felt the sensation of melting. Of melting and flowing as an integral part of space-time, for want of a better phrase. I was an atomic drop of liquid poured into a river without beginning, end or embankments. Perfection was an empty, archaic word to me. I had never thought it could be intellectually employed, and I was especially careful not to apply it to that shifting abstract—woman. I was looking at it now. A perfect woman. A creation molded from centuries of perfection; a creation of symmetric loveliness that was literally and figuratively out of this world.

My last day on Earth was ended. I had opened my eyes. I saw first that some miracle of science had reconstructed the burned away half of my right arm. Then I noticed the woman. I was sitting bolt upright in an instant on the smooth metal table. The little man with his strange "Buck Rogers" dress was looking quietly at me. And she was looking at me, too, out of slitted lids that veiled all the women of the ages in subtly yet violently burning eyes.

She lifted a jeweled hand. Her sensual lips trembled a little before they parted, and strong white teeth gleamed provocatively between the red lines.

I started, and gripped hard at the edges of the table. Was this the way a woman scientist studied coldly and objectively a prospective laboratory subject? I looked questioningly at the little wizened man who had kidnaped me from my own world. His blank face showed me nothing.

Then, when she spoke....

I don't want to take unnecessary time at this point or any other to explain or describe this woman, Jokan. I doubt if you could visualize her anyway, even if I occupied this entire narrative describing her, because she was too strangely lovely. She was perfection, as I've said, and that's all. Her voice was music, and I involuntarily started toward her as she spoke.

"Withdraw the brain recorder, Draken," she said softly, not taking those icy eyes from mine. The little man, Draken, complied. She pointed to a great three-dimensional chart extending across the laboratory. It was made up of shifting convolutions and numerical graphs and complicated combinations of shadings corresponding to brain patterns.

"That is your brain, Ivan," she said. Her voice was cold, completely frozen, and yet—"We know all about you." I felt a little disappointment along with the relief. She turned toward Draken.

"You made a great mistake, Draken. Bringing in an Intellectual was a foolish thing to do."

Draken objected. "But you said you wanted a good physical specimen. This man is. You defined your requested specimen in no greater detail."

"But you should know that an intellectual can cause difficulties. This man would be considered a god among the women. Perhaps even among the men. Mohln is at a point where such an element as this could precipitate disaster, create perhaps a germ of dissatisfaction with our great order. Or is that, by chance, what you intend?"

Draken backed away. "No, it isn't."

"Don't let the presence of this man be known beyond these four walls, or out of your own laboratory. For your sake and mine, heed my suggestion, Draken."

"Yes," quivered Draken. "I am heeding it. But you know my attitude toward this *great* order. You know how I regard the maintenance of the Status Quo."

I knew it too, from the way his pallid lips curled. This little man hated the Mohln system, whatever it was.

Jokan got languidly to her feet, a fluid musical allegro. "I know, Draken. If you weren't the greatest thinker in Mohln besides myself, I would report you to the Council for the Maintenance of the Status Quo. But as long as you only think idly, you can cause Mohln no harm."

"The only harm Mohln can suffer," said Draken wearily, "is to continue on as it does now. Toward final decay and rot."

Jokan laughed frostily. I shivered. "Stop worrying, Draken, and go away. I must begin my experiments." She turned her eyes on me. She could have stared down a bronze statue. I turned my eyes from hers on the pretense of looking for Draken, but he was gone.

I jumped to my feet, and the movement revealed that I, too, had on the costume that Draken wore.

Without egoism, I can say that it must have looked more becoming on me than on the little scientist. I was at least a foot taller than Jokan.

She came toward me, fluid motion. I couldn't back away—I insist I wanted to get away for various reasons, the least being that I wanted to get solid on my mental feet—from the metal table. I looked almost frantically for a door or some kind of exit, even a window. There was nothing.

Then those perfect arms slipped around my neck and that body pressed itself against mine and—

I am only human. That's a trite enough excuse, if an excuse is necessary, but under those conditions I could certainly do no less. I let my arms come around her perfect waist, and I bent her back in the most acceptable televex manner and planted a long solid one right on those perfect lips—lips I'm very certain had never been kissed before.

And that was precisely the trouble, perhaps, with that thoughtless, but irresistible, impulse of mine. Her nails were long and sharp and they clawed at my face. Cold light blazed in her eyes, flashing with outraged dignity and burning hate.

I swung down and away, sliding across the metal table, and stood with blood running down my face, with the table my only protection between myself and this paradoxical Circe.

"Savage," she shrieked, and shrieking was very unbecoming to the cold austerity of her. In fact it was like a cloak I had torn away from her body. "Primal, barbaric beast!"

"I'm not quite primal enough to cope with you," I said, looking more frantically still for an exit. There still weren't any exits, but people came into this room, and people went out of it. How?

I expected her to vault the table after me, but she lithely backed away, and though I didn't realize it then, her cold brain was summoning her eunuchs from afar.

A section of the wall to one side began to glow like a light through semi-opaque glass. The light deepened and began to whirl. And then I saw that there was a kind of opening there. Yes. A kind of opening with something promising no good lumbering through, its head and massive shoulders projecting up out of the shifting mist like a televexed fictional monster.

It was a monstrous metal man. A real, animated robot out of an old scientification fabrication. It was coming directly for me. I flashed one look—I think it was a beseeching one—at Jokan. In such instances as that people swallow great lumps of their pride.

Jokan was stretched up to her complete height against the far wall. Her face was expressionless, and her eyes oozed liquid oxygen. Her hands were strained into fists at her sides. "Atavistic," Draken had said of this female scientist of Mohln. An understatement promising no hope for consideration.

I dodged beneath the robot's reaching appendages. There were three arms with a number of variously utilized digits at the end of each. And all of them were wicked. Many of them designed for purposes I couldn't grasp. Anyway I looked at it, the robot represented a perfect mauling and crushing instrument.

I can describe it now with a light touch. *Then* I was trembling with cold fear, and sweat poured off my face as I eluded the robot by dodging about the only fixture in the middle of the room, the table. I noticed a minor motion of Jokan; then I watched, with a hideously empty stomach, the table fold itself into the floor.

I leaped to one side and grabbed Jokan, twisted her around in front of me, and said with as little chattering as possible into her perfect pink little ear, "Call them off or—"

I tightened my arm about her throat and began bending her head back. She writhed around and kicked me, and her finger nails started their old habit pattern again. But she wasn't used to this sort of thing, and didn't employ any real effeminate technique at all.

I continued bending her head back. I could feel her choking and gasping. She knew then that I would kill her. I hadn't asked to come to Mohln, wherever and whenever it was. It was all something I had nothing to do with, that now threatened my life. All directly the responsibility of Jokan. To me, she was a real Circe, deserving no sympathy, only hate, and deserving death. But I could never have actually tried, or threatened to kill her, under less pressing conditions than those. It was simply a case of breaking her neck to save mine, which I consider justified.

The metallic digits squeezed shut on each elbow, from behind. I twisted my head upward at the second robot, sweating pain in my eyes. Unfeeling paralysis then, as the digits tore through muscle tendon, nerve fibers and even cracked bone. I was mouthing sounds, probably screaming, hearing my own cries from a great distance, blinded by pain, a mist blurring my eyes.

I was lifted straight up, then swung down beneath one implacable arm. I dangled there, my crushed elbows swinging and dripping beneath my face. I saw those perfect little feet come up and stand in front of my tortured eyes. And they *were* perfect little feet, encased in red sandals to match the blood from my wounds. Even facing torture, and possible death, I thought of them as perfect little feet. I didn't attempt to twist my face upward.

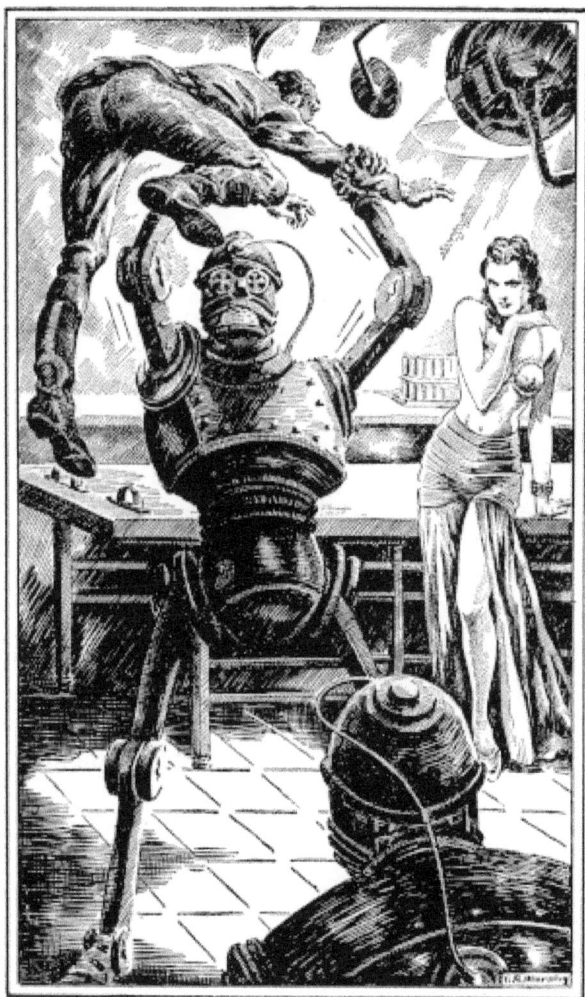

I kept on staring crazily at those perfect little feet. There was character and expression in them, different and more sympathetic than the body they supported. They came closer, shifted a bit, uncertain and nervous. I had been brought here as the subject for anatomical research, a laboratory specimen to be dissected. Yet, for an instant, another purpose had shown in Jokan's eyes. I knew that, or did I merely want to know it. I tried to imagine how terribly lonely and maladjusted she must be in a loveless world. Beautiful and to be desired, yet in a loveless, sexless world.

With specimens like Draken, I could easily guess that this was the kind of world in which Jokan lived out frustration. Perfect women, and pathetic, skin-and-bone puppets for men.

She had said I would be a god among women. Without egoism, again, I could see why. There was too much gross ambiguity. The women and men just didn't seem to be of identical species. And in addition, Jokan was an atavistic.

Which wouldn't matter anymore to me, because I was being dragged out of there. Where? Into what? How could I know? I watched those feet fade into blurred distance. They were whirling around as they faded. I knew I was losing all grasp of consciousness. Which was all right, too, because hard after the initial shock, the real excruciating agony was beginning to shoot into my brain.

Only a few hours later, that's all, and I was all in one piece again. A more effective and healthy feeling organism than before, thanks to incredible biological treatments I couldn't even guess at. I kept flexing my arms, watching them bend and unbend with questioning fascination.

I turned toward Draken. "Why am I still here and alive?"

Draken's embryonic face puckered at me like an impish child's.

He explained: "Jokan is an atavist as I said. Women have always been noted for their bodies rather than their brains, although potentially their brain capacity has always been equal to the male's. And that cultural error has never been changed. Instead, women have grown more beautiful and symmetrical with the centuries, from the standpoint of decadent and ancient aesthetic values. The men, on the other hand, have always been considered as thinkers rather than as creations of beauty. They have developed brain potential alone, while their physical characteristics have atrophied.

"Except for atavists like Jokan, the overly curious longing for the male body, as you represent it, has been conditioned out of the reaction patterns by the psycho-medics by centuries of selection. Jokan, as you have seen, is different. She demanded that I go back to your time, or even further back and return with a man capable of matching her body in physical attraction.

You enraged her for a moment, but she has recovered from that momentary emotional unbalance."

I objected at this point. "But you said I was to be just a laboratory specimen for dissection."

"This whole transaction was elaborate and demanded official sanction from the Council. So, on the record, your space-time teleportation is only for biological purposes. You understand."

I nodded. It was not an exceptional situation, basically. It seemed that a few million years of evolution can't destroy the fundamental behavior patterns entirely. "A good man's still hard to find?"

The little scientist stared in blank affirmation. Then he said: "I could have chosen any number of men who could have satisfied Jokan's demands, perhaps even more thoroughly than you. Don't you wonder why I singled you out? With your background in your world, and your ideological concepts, you were the only one for me to chose—for my own purposes."

"Which are—" I prompted.

"Neither of the preceding purposes are the basic ones for my asking you to return here with me. The real reason is that you must destroy Mohln."

I stared. I turned everything over in my mind, then tried to say calmly: "Why? This is civilization and the apex of human progress for which I face death daily in my own time. Destroy it!"

I had begun to regard this little withered man as a first class fanatic, born of highly complicated and advanced psychological conflicts.

He said: "When the Earth was enveloped in its final ice sheet, living as we demanded it ceased to be feasible. The pick of human mentality and physiognomy migrated here to Mohln. Here we began our great—what we thought great—new and scientific social order. Yes, it's reached a zenith all right. A zenith of decay and stagnation. Except for a few scientists, Mohln is populated by mindless automatons. Beautiful, mindless women, and great brained, spineless men. They all exist in a futile vacuum."

I was watching him narrowly for signs of madness. He looked mad enough, but his squeezed up face was unreadable. I said feebly: "From what little experience I've had here, you seem to have reached a pretty ultimate state of civilization."

"That is the great tragedy. There is no ultimate state. That is the great delusion which you must shatter. Everyone, societies, worlds, all seek an ultimate state. Change is the law, and there is no ultimate law. This world of Mohln thinks it has achieved an ultimate perfection. It has, because of the delusion, only succeeded in stagnation. This social structure is neither alive nor dead, Ivan Allinger. It is standing still. The ultimate futility is to be static."

"Then you refute yourself," I said, feeling for a sophistic insert. "You have reached an ultimate something."

"Only movement is the ultimate goal. And change is success. Advancement—progress is limitless. This culture of Mohln has reached an ultimate lostness. Only one action can shake it back onto the pattern of change. The entire World-City of Mohln must be destroyed, reduced to chaos. Out of this chaos, by trial and error, the people of Mohln must be given the germ of incentive again, and forced by necessity to fight their way back onto new roads of endeavor."

I thought hard. I felt familiar struggles in my heart. I understood this. My own life was dedicated, back in my own space and time, to this same effort and goal—to stimulate progress, and change; to destroy all reactionary elements that might lead to permanence.

He followed my introspection with words. "You fought in the great wars of your time against the reactionary forces that would have led your society into staticism and decay. You are devoting the present to the furthering of the ideals of progress. Do you want to see all your work, and all the work of all your kind, of your own present, past and future end in—this?"

He spread his withered arms about him, encompassing the whole of the World-City of Mohln.

"No," I heard myself muttering. "No. I wouldn't want that. I would prevent it, if I could. But I demand more than your words to convince me that this magnificence of organization I see about me is the hopeless futility you are telling me it is."

"I will take you out into the city and show you," he said. "But it is strictly against the rules of the Council. And the few intellectuals, the scientists and research technicians don't care anymore about the disintegration of the order about them. In their own little worlds they find something to work on, a stimulus, and they ignore everything else. Like Jokan."

Draken led me out onto a balcony, and I saw—well, a word that might inspire somewhat explanatory suggestive visions of what I saw, in your own mind, could be the symbol, Utopia. It was an endlessly stretching composite of all social dreams.

The mauve lighting that softened the city like a beautiful mist. The mighty, gleaming plastic shells of buildings. Power hung at levels reaching high toward a translucent dome that covered the city. Tiers on tiers of splendidly designed walkways, tubeways and highways networked the spaces between structures. And the air sang with music, more magnificent than all the symphonies of my own time.

I forgot the dizzying height, and almost stepped out into the exalting splendor of it. There seemed no danger, as though it were all an endless soft cloud of enchantment into which I could sink, then float buoyed up by dreams and music and shifting light....

But the little tugging fingers of Draken dragged me back.

"It is all false," he whispered. "It is all delusion. Beneath all this grandeur the lost puppets dance and sleep, but never live. These words, which are the only words that make a social system worthy of continuation— curiosity, incentive, ambition, drive, longing, dissatisfaction—all meaningless here, all unknown to these pathetic tropisms. If you will come with me, you can see for yourself, and understand."

I went with little Draken. I did see for myself. I understood....

And Draken was entirely correct in all that he had said. This World-City of Mohln had achieved an ultimate—an ultimate lostness. It was a magnificent hollow shell of a City. There were no people in it. All the mighty wonder was lost to the semi-living marionettes that wandered through it. But it meant life to them, nevertheless. They never had to exert a finger, nor expend the energy of one thousandth of a gram of thinking energy to live. But the technocratic creations of long preceding times, of even a few still working scientists, kept them alive. But they neither knew this, nor cared.

They were fed, clothed, bathed and even reborn by robots. They were put to sleep, awakened, vitalized, and exhausted by machines. They were parasitic non-entities, dependent on the machines that other, *vital* minds, had built.

Back on the balcony, Draken continued in that squeaky, uncertain quaver of his:

"Everything here is done by robots. There are different castes of robots. Their functional system is graduated up through ever lessening numbers until it reaches what is only a master switch. One single switch in this World-City, pushed too far—" Draken looked at me suggestively and added hoarsely:

"If the master switch was ever pushed too far, this entire civilization, as you call it, would stop functioning with any set mechanical pattern. All the robots and machines and the system they operate would cease activity. There would be your chaos. There would be the needed situation under which the unthinking slaves will have to think for themselves, solve their own problems once again. Or die. I think they will solve them. I have that much faith in them. They always have. So far."

It was a statement on Draken's part. But it was really a question. Would I push that master switch—too far?

"Why haven't *you* done this before?" I asked. "Why drag a man from another world, a million years in the past, to do this simple thing?"

Draken lowered his head in the first display of real, understandable emotion I had seen in him. Shame. "I can't," he said simply. "I do not have the will, the free will to do it. My intellect tells me it is the correct thing to do. But my psycho-conditioning has created an insurmountable antipathy toward such an act."

His dried up monkey-like hands clenched into tiny impotent fists. "Many times I have gone into that room and tried to pull that switch. But each time I have failed. I know now that I shall never be able to. No one in this world could do it until you came. You can. Your age was a dynamic one, of destruction and construction, each inseparable from the other. You could do it, not only with ease, but with the satisfaction of knowing you were taking a necessary step forward in human progress. The question is—will you?"

———————————————

A lot of time clambered through my fogged mind then before I formulated a logical sequence of thoughts that led to what seemed to me a logical reply.

"I believe I will," I finally answered slowly. "I can't see that there is any other way out."

"Execution," a familiarly brittle voice said behind me, and I turned. Draken began whimpering pathetically and cowered back against the colonnade.

Jokan stood a few feet from me, wearing a thin, semi-transparent gown that seemed anachronistic and out of place, as though she had gotten the idea for it out of an old history book. Her body was a lithe shadow behind it. But her eyes burned irrascible hatred.

"Execution for you, and for Draken; that is a better way."

"I wish I could agree," I said. "But you see our concern is for society as a whole, rather than with a small minority that benefit from the apathy and ignorance of the majority. For your satisfaction, and that of a few others, you may be right. Frankly, dear Jokan, though you're very very lovely to look at, your mind is ugly and warped. And I would rather see you dead."

I sprang and reached for her. She screamed once, before the robots came in and lumbered for me. I remember mumbling about the monotony of the robot act; as she eluded me, and I eluded them. And I kept on trying to grab Jokan. It was an obsession with me.

A quick glance revealed Draken cowered down in his corner, his old child's face twisted in stunned horror.

My only intention at that moment was to get my hands around Jokan's perfect neck just one more time. It was a mad, fanatical urge now. I hated her. I hated her with a blind madness.

The robots weren't nearly as dexterous as they should have been. Physical encounter was undoubtedly alien to their primary purpose. This place of Draken's was bigger, with a few articles in it, than the laboratory had been. There were pneumatic chairs and couches and ray lamps and vitamin globes. I ducked, sprawled, ran and careened in and out of these rooms and around the strange looking fixtures. I, close on Jokan's sandaled heels, and the robots close on mine. It might even seem more or less a comical scene in retrospect, but—

Then I saw that silver sphere of Draken's, hanging in the air about four feet from the floor, smooth, mysterious, but very suggestive. As I ran back past Draken, I yelled at him.

I doubt if Draken understood my words, he was so stricken with horror, but he grasped my meaning, and somehow managed to stagger onto his quavering legs and tottered wild-eyed toward the sphere.

But Jokan understood my meaning, too. And through some telepathic direction I still don't understand, she guided the robots onto poor Draken. Draken never had a chance.

I don't think he even comprehended conflict. He could neither fight back, nor try to escape. It seemed that violence, either offensive or defensive, was beyond his understanding. That was why he could not bring himself to pull the master switch that would have accomplished his desired destruction of Mohln. That was also the reason why the robot was able to take him into its inexorable metal arms and crush him into something not far removed from pulp.

His delicate, deep pocketed eyes looked beseechingly into mine, once. Then the tremendous pressure bulged them horribly and unconsciously at me. His bony arms flapped and waved spasmodically and blood spurted from his small almost invisible ears and equally minute nose. Then his whole frail body seemed to crack through the middle and deflate. At another telepathic command from Jokan, the robot's arms raised and unbent, and the body of Draken thudded on the inlaid floor.

I heard myself yelling. I wasn't retreating from the other two robots then, or trying to get away at all. Something gave way inside me. What I had seen just now shocked every sense that might have been ethical or moral in me. One word churned inside my brain. The word was revenge. And then another word was added to it that seemed better. Compensation. Then another word etched in capital letters overshadowed and encompassed the other two. *Kill.*

The first robot reached out with its very utilitarian and gadget-studded arms to rake me in. I had no idea how much the monster weighed. But the Frankensteinian creation was off balance as it reached for me. I twisted and grasped the metalic tentacle, heaved forward, throwing my hip into the gleaming stomach and heaved down.

The robot seemed light-weighted enough as it flew ceilingward, and clanged hollowly against the wall. There was a flash of current, a slight odor of ozone as the teleo-electronic man twitched about at my feet.

The violence evidently stunned my fair and wicked Circe. Her telepathic control over the remaining robots faltered and in that instant I seized her. A dead, hot rage swelled through my head and heart so I could hardly draw a breath. I wrenched at her neck, felt it crack dangerously and felt her long sleek muscles tremble against mine.

I felt almost bestial in the power of my rage. I twisted sidewise and felt her body give, and heard her breath coming in short jagged whines like a dog's. Her finger nails weren't clawing now. The cold, emotionless cruelty of her eyes was dying behind fear and indecision. She hadn't been reluctant to dream of blood and guts and shattered bones, but too much of the real thing hurt even her atavistic senses.

"Keep them off me," I said in her ear. She tried to pull away. I held her at arm's length and began slapping her. Her face was white as powder until red finger marks appeared on it. I hit harder and her perfect upper lip split and a narrow line of blood ran down and stained the dark hollow between her perfect marble breasts. The gold-flecked pupils of her eyes widened, and the horror deepened in back of them. The the horror went out like a flame and the lids with the perfect long lashes blinked over them and tears flowed down as from a weeping statue.

I threw a quick circuit about the room. The robots were immobile; tensed, though, for action. At any moment Jokan might regain her Circe faculties and summon them, even if it meant her own life. I didn't know then what emotions surged around inside her strange heart. I lifted her onto my shoulder and started through the rooms.

I had no idea how to escape. Whatever inconceivable manner the walls dissolved through the manipulation of incredible advanced force fields, I of course didn't know. But I put three rooms filled with the futuristic mores between myself and the robot minions of Jokan before I dropped her on a pneumatic couch and wrapped my hands about her throat for the third time and began to squeeze.

I began slowly and methodically, looking all the time into her eyes. Then I saw it. I saw the real depths of her eyes, and a shock trembled through me. Jokan had changed. How she had changed!

She read the implacable purpose in my eyes that I felt in my heart, and as her arms came up, mine slid down softly from about her throat. I kissed her. I lifted her passive softness up and felt it respond. The hands with the feral nails caressed the back of my neck, and her lips were hungry.

I had seen in her eyes a change, and had answered it. Then I said: "Lead me to the room that holds the master switch. Then we'll go."

She slid out of my arms languidly and onto her feet. She leaned toward me, and her fingers grasped mine. They were warm, not cold; how could they ever have been cold? "Go where?"

"Can you run that space-time apparatus that brought me here?"

She nodded, then looked fearfully over my face.

"Take me to the main switch," I repeated.

We went back, and she somehow attracted the translucent, yet not translucent, sphere to her side. It followed after her like a monstrous being, a cosmic slave.

She led me toward the wall and it dissolved. I still am not able to understand the phenomenon. We continued through and into an elevator. We dropped down through a blur of distance. She led me through a glowing tunnel and into a tubecar and there was a dim sensation of movement in which we might have sped a thousand miles, or ten thousand.

She led me out of the tubecar and we crossed a walkway, where lines of listless people stood moving in various directions. The little swollen-headed men and the tall austere but listless women. They were all going places, but it didn't matter. They had eyes, ears, senses, but they might have been machines reacting through photo-electric devices. I thirsted for the main switch that would send them all into blind chaos. It was a hellish thing for the world I had risked my life many times to build upward and progressively toward greatness. But it had all ended here, a blind alley of despair, and the hell I planned would be its only salvation.

Suddenly, from all sides, robots converged on us, directed by a number of the little white-skulled men with velvet togas flapping about slug-white spindly legs.

"The Council," said Jokan. "They are afraid now. They attack, and they are half mad because they have been conditioned that such an act of violence is atavism, the inexcusable social crime."

Their puckered faces, in the center of the bloated domes of heads, were strained and flinching. The robots shambled onto Jokan and me, and Jokan did something to them with her mind which evidently was more powerful in this capacity at least than all the Council combined. And the robots turned and began flailing each other into lumps of smoking twisted metal.

My stomach crawled. The Council, supreme intellects of a million years of progress, had fallen down onto the moving walkway, slobbering and twitching in the final stages of dementia. Even a thousand gram brain breaks when faced with an insolvable problem. The gleaming expanse of moving plastic carried the Council out of our sight. The little men and the Amazonian women who slouched past didn't even notice. And if they did, it was foreign to their conditioning. They couldn't think about it.

They would soon have to think. When I pushed the master switch too far....

We encountered no more resistance, if that feeble expression of the apex of human development so far met could be called resistance. Finally we emerged into a room that surprised me with its lack of grandeur and its barrenness. All the World-City that was meaningless was a dream of ostentation and color and beauty of intricate design. This room, in contrast, the heart of the World-City, the key to its life, was completely denuded. A small plastic shell and in the middle was a conical dais and on the dais was a lever.

Jokan nodded toward the lever and her eyes that followed me as I walked to it and moved it, were bright with some inner fire I couldn't diagnose.

I jerked my hand away.

The meaning of my act enveloped me in a mist of fear. I trembled violently. Sweat beaded on my face and smarted in my eyes.

Had I been right in my choice? Had Draken been correct in his analysis, and had I been justified in jumping to such an empirical conclusion without more conclusive proof? Had all these nameless slaves of decay been victims of the delusion from which I had freed them? Or had I been deluded by the lies of a fanatic?

I looked down and saw my hand reaching for the lever to move it back. It was an unconscious gesture motivated by vague fears. I seemed such a little man to destroy a world.

What was happening to all animated puppets of this future society now that its mechanical contrivances had been destroyed? What had happened, even back in my own time, in large cities, when only the electric systems had been blown up, or the water mains, or gas mains? What mind-numbing chaos and madness must be developing around me as I stood inside the heart of a world which I had torn loose from its arteries.

Jokan led me from the room and onto a balcony. Somehow I had thought myself down far in the bowels of this World-City. But as I stepped out, clouds were on a level with my eyes, synthetic clouds, and wind slapped my face. We looked down.

Blind in that room with only my imaginative thoughts, the vastness of my act had been a conceivable thing. Here, looking over the true vastness, an endlessness, I found my brain whirling, refusing to consider what was really happening. In a monody of sadness and fatalism, Jokan recited the meaning to me, as she watched her world crumble.

A sound surged up and about me. A low murmuring that grew and expanded into a vibrating roar. To my right, far away, I saw a massive steely structure explode into a billion fragments and a blinding flash of power carried to my ears a splitting roar. It began happening all over, through the tiers and levels and towering heights of the World-City, as far on any side I looked, as far as I could see.

I cringed. Below, a sea of blind ants scurried madly about in infantile terror. Flying boats crashed as their automatic pilots stopped functioning. All the power of the city had ceased. The smoothly working machinery had become an onrushing nemesis of destruction, each stride feeding on the preceding flaw in function or the complete lack of any function.

Huge structures, power-hung, dropped their millions of tons of weight onto hordes of milling humans who had no idea what was happening—if they had ever known.

Gravity neutralizing units died and whole tiers collapsed. Unlimited power from the harnessing of liquid oxygen reversed into a destructive titan; a wave of overpowering heat rose up in a choking mist. Then the building on which we stood began to tremble.

I turned. The bobbing sphere of escape was between Jokan and I, a small supremely compact unit of atomic power, perhaps, conducting its own motivation. "Why doesn't it stop, too?" I asked, as people ask ambiguous questions in a crisis.

"It responds to the human mind alone," she said. "We have progressed far in physiogenics, too, as well as in the mechanical sciences. Perhaps it is the real world after all. We can go far beyond the machines."

"We'd better go someplace—fast," I said shakily, for the building lurched sickeningly, and I toppled back against the wall. The colonnade buckled in front of me, but Jokan wasn't afraid. She kept looking over the World-City.

I stumbled toward her. The heat was intensifying, becoming intolerable. I clutched at her frantically. "You are going with me," I shouted. I doubt if she heard me. "I love you," I yelled into her ear. "Don't you understand?" She heard that. Her lips smiled thinly. Pain altered her face like a plastic mask.

I felt the gigantic power of the sphere then as before. It began to glow and oscillate and expand. And it sucked me into its limitless depths and cosmological labyrinths as before. I felt the melting and flowing and the indescribable twisted warping of sanity....

Jokan, working at my side, has done much to conquer the evil virus of the Spartan menace. Her scientific knowledge, and her telepathic acumen, place her above many of our greatest minds. This is enhanced by an almost fanatical desire to destroy those who would destroy social progress. Her faithfulness to duty is legendary.

We love each other with ties no one can understand who hesitate to conceive of bonds extending through dimensions of space and time. She never leaves my side in the unceasing night and day, crusading against the Fascistic disease that is being stamped out, though painfully and with aching slowness, that has extended over six centuries.

But between us there is an uneasiness. Sometimes this uneasiness finds expression in little episodes—like the conversation at the last meeting of the International Agencies in Casablanca. We were having drinks before going into the Presidium.

Jokan was lovely—that's a dismal understatement—in a low cut evening gown of plasti-silk. Her eyes were half closed.

"Will we ever win?" she said over the brim of a Tom Collins, which is still the world's favorite cocktail.

"Yes," I said. Then I turned casually, though I didn't feel casual at all. I knew what she was thinking.

"You must be the greatest optimist of all time," she said. "And I'll help you and myself and all of us stay that way. I'll never mention it again. Perhaps we can both forget."

"Try to forget what?" I said, though I knew well enough.

Her eyes fixed mine as only her eyes can. "Forget that the great world we're fighting so hard to build we will be destroying a million years from tonight."

I coughed and ordered another drink for myself. But I can't forget.

Milton Keynes UK
Ingram Content Group UK Ltd.
UKHW030627061024
449204UK00004B/237

9 789362 517395